MEMBERS ONLY

Fabrice Roger-Lacan
MEMBERS ONLY

Translated by
Christopher Campbell

OBERON BOOKS
LONDON

First published in this translation in 2006 by Oberon Books Ltd
Electronic edition published in 2012

Oberon Books Ltd
521 Caledonian Road, London N7 9RH
Tel: 020 7607 3637 / Fax: 020 7607 3629
e-mail: info@oberonbooks.com
www.oberonbooks.com

A catalogue record for this book is available from the British Library.

Cover photograph by Steve Ullathorne

PB ISBN: 978-1-84002-661-0
E ISBN: 978-1-84943-788-2

eBook conversion by Replika Press PVT Ltd, India.

Characters

BERNARD

ADRIEN

Note Words in italics in square brackets are not spoken. They indicate what the character might have said, had they continued speaking.

This translation was first produced on 28 March 2006 at Trafalgar Studios, London, by Coup de Théâtre and Emmenez-Nous au Théâtre, with the following cast:

BERNARD, Robert Bathurst
ADRIEN, Nicolas Tennant

Director, Marianne Badrichani
Associate Director, Sarah Davey
Designer, Vicki Fifield
Lighting Designer, Tony Simpson
Sound Designer, Daniel Biro
Company Stage Manager, Rebecca Maltby
Co-Producers ENAT, Sandra Soudry & Nathalie Berrebi
Associate Producer, Eleanor Lloyd
Photographers, Steve Ullathorne & Simon Annand
Publicity Design, Pete Le May

Scene 1

An office. An architect's studio. Two work-tables facing each other. BERNARD surges in, humming happily. He picks up the phone and dials...

BERNARD: Hello Babette, darling... It's me, it's Daddy... Thank you, poppet... You've made me a birthday present...? A drawing? A picture of me? 'Picture', sweetheart, not pixture, 'pic-ture'... You bet I want to see it! ... Can you put Mummy on? ... What? ... I'm forty... Well, I gather I was born around ten o'clock at night, quite late anyway... No, you're absolutely right, I'm not quite forty yet... Hmm? ... Well, it's not old and it's not young, it's in the middle... The middle, the middle of life... No it doesn't necessarily mean that I'll die forty years from today... 'Dead', darling, not 'deaded'... I don't know, maybe sooner maybe later, we just don't know with things like that, darling, you're a big girl, you know that... Because we just can't... Now, why are you crying? ... No, I'm not going to die, why would you want to say that? ... Chicky... I'm not saying you want me to die... No, I know you don't... Dry your eyes, my chick, my little angel, I'm fit as a fiddle, I'm a sort of mega-super-fit superdaddio and I'm going to live such a long, long time that one day you'll be absolutely fed up with me hanging about the place! ... I'm kidding, treasure... Yes, I'll be home very, very soon, any minute now, put Mummy on... Kiss kiss...kiss kiss, kiss kiss, kiss kiss... Put Mum... Yes, kiss kiss, come on now... All right, we'll do the big count down. Stand by: five...four...three...two...one... Kiss kiss! (*Pause. His voice changes.*) Yeah, hi there... Nothing... No, I didn't tell her off... Yes. Well, it's in the bag, we've signed... How d'you know? ... Where did you bump into him?

... And he really said that? ... Two-faced bastard, he must be seething... You're telling me it's fantastic! ... Everything, we got the lot... No, well done Adrien, it's all his work... Well, yes, it's both of us, but it's him who's been having lunch with the Committee top bananas every day for the last three months... No, he's on his way... I'll tell him... Love you... Yes, it's a hell of a birthday present... You haven't asked anyone round tonight, have you? ... Just the family... Just the five of us. Perfect... Love you... (*He hangs up.*)

BERNARD goes off into an adjoining wash-room to get a bottle of champagne. We hear footsteps and BERNARD hides.

Enter ADRIEN...

ADRIEN: Bernard...?

He puts down his motorbike helmet and a bag of clothes from the dry-cleaners. He sits down with his feet up on his desk and a smile on his face.

BERNARD: (*Bursting out.*) Dadah!

He fires the champagne cork towards ADRIEN.

ADRIEN: Argh! Oh, fuck it, my eye!

BERNARD: It just missed you.

ADRIEN: It got me right in the eye!

BERNARD: It didn't...

ADRIEN: It did! That really hurts!

BERNARD: Let's see... I know you're having me on...

ADRIEN: Ow, ow, ow! It feels like a detached retina!

BERNARD: Give over… (*Goes over to him.*) Let's have a look…

ADRIEN: They're bastards, those corks…

BERNARD: Take your hand away, let me see it…

BERNARD bends over him, ADRIEN jerks upright with a yell. BERNARD jumps back in shock.

ADRIEN: Had you going…!

BERNARD: Not even a little bit.

ADRIEN: Oh yeah, sure…

BERNARD: I called Léo to tell her the news. She sends her love and says well done…

He pours champagne for them both and hands ADRIEN a glass. They clink glasses and drink. BERNARD refills the glasses.

She bumped into Chicamour at tennis. He already knew. He told her to pass on his 'congratulations' to me.

ADRIEN: That's nice. Pretty gracious of him really…

BERNARD: You're calling Roland Chicamour 'gracious'.

ADRIEN: Doing the decent thing.

BERNARD: Now look. You can plead extenuating circumstances for anyone you like, but not for Chicamour!

ADRIEN: 'Extenuating circumstances'? We're not… [*in court.*]

BERNARD: Ten years I've been doing this job, and for ten years this guy has been royally shafting me every time I…

ADRIEN: It's called being a competitor.

BERNARD: A competitor? Chicamour? A fair competitor?

ADRIEN: We hand out little presents as well.

BERNARD: Yes, little presents. Not... Chicamour is a sleaze-merchant. A sleaze-merchant and an orgiast.

ADRIEN: Maybe so. I don't really see...

BERNARD: Is he or is he not a sleaze-merchant?

ADRIEN: Look, did Chicamour get this contract or did we? Why are you getting worked up?

BERNARD: It's you! You blur everything. I'm sorry, there are the good guys and there are the sleaze-merchants.

ADRIEN: (*He's heard it before.*) ...and if it wasn't for the sleaze-merchants there wouldn't be any good guys...

BERNARD: Yes there would. Evil exists! You don't want to see it but it's there.

ADRIEN: Where?! (*He's relaxed and not in the mood to get into this argument.*)

BERNARD: Okay, all right... (*He raises his glass.*) Here's to you! Great work!

ADRIEN: To you!

They clink glasses and drink, smiling at each other.
BERNARD refills the glasses.

BERNARD: To your irresistible charm, your dangerously contagious enthusiasm and...your total lack of scruples...

ADRIEN: I thank you.

They drink, then ADRIEN lifts his glass.

To your tenacity, your very particular…exactitude, and your pathological touchiness.

BERNARD smiles. They drink. Pause. BERNARD frowns.

BERNARD: You think I'm touchy?

ADRIEN: Aren't you?

BERNARD: I dunno.

ADRIEN: You really think I've no scruples?

BERNARD: I was joking. I just mean you go for it, that's all…but I can tell you do actually think I'm touchy.

ADRIEN: Well you are a bit. I mean, look at you now…

BERNARD: What? You've just accused me of being touchy, that's really annoying!

ADRIEN: Okay, okay, let's call it… Okay, I drink to your exquisite sensitivity…your flower-like sensibility! How's that for you? Sounds nice… Come on…

They drink. BERNARD raises his glass.

BERNARD: To the two of us! And the very special bond which unites us!

He refills ADRIEN's glass and makes to fill his own.

ADRIEN: You'll be putting a fair bit of that away tonight.

BERNARD: What do you mean?

ADRIEN: I don't know…just, it's your birthday…

BERNARD: There's nothing arranged…

ADRIEN: You'll have a celebration at home though…

BERNARD: I'm not really in the habit of necking litres of champagne with Léo and the girls.

ADRIEN: I'm sure you'll have a little glass...

BERNARD: Aha! ... What a give-away! Léo's set up a surprise party!

ADRIEN: No, no, what do you mean...?

BERNARD: Oh, yes, don't you lie to me...

ADRIEN: I'm telling you!

BERNARD: Telling me what?

ADRIEN: That...nothing... Léo hasn't set up anything... I don't know anything about it anyway...

BERNARD: You're lying to me, Adrien...

ADRIEN: I'm not!

BERNARD: You are lying to your friend and business partner!

ADRIEN: What makes you think...?

BERNARD: Stop it! Stop. It tears me up that you can lie to me. Even though it's in fun, it just tears me up...

ADRIEN: Look, I swear to you...

BERNARD: Stop it, I'm serious about this, don't swear... Anyway I knew about it already, Babette gave the game away... Don't worry about it.

ADRIEN: I don't know what you're talking about.

BERNARD: (*Explodes.*) Stop it, Adrien, for fuck's sake! I've just told you I know about it. Léo has laid on a surprise fortieth birthday party for me tonight! I know all about it.

Pause.

ADRIEN: Does Léo know you know?

BERNARD: I reckon she does know I know, but because I'm pretending I don't know she's pretending she doesn't know I know...

ADRIEN: That's brilliant!

BERNARD: What is?

ADRIEN: You two! The two of you and the girls, the whole thing! It's so what you're good at... It's like... It's a vocation... It's brilliant!

BERNARD: Is this irony?

ADRIEN: It's envy... If my wife had ever arranged a surprise party for me...and she never would have... but if my wife had taken it into her head to lay on something like that and then if I'd found out...well, forget it... It's just there are some people who have more of a gift for being happy than others...

BERNARD: That's a bit glib.

ADRIEN: No really...

BERNARD: You got married when you were twenty-five to a pain in the arse, that's all. Could happen to anyone.

ADRIEN: Not to you.

BERNARD: Because I was lucky...

ADRIEN: That's what I'm saying...it's a gift. Mozart was 'lucky' he could compose his first symphony when he was six and a half...

BERNARD: But after that he put in the work like everyone else, maybe a lot more than everyone else.

ADRIEN: So?

BERNARD: I'm just saying it's a bit too easy to put your hands up like that and leave it to everyone else to keep the wheels of copulation turning and propagate the species.

Silence.

ADRIEN: Are you telling me that everything you've built up with Léo, your relationship, the kids, the house, the home… You've done all this with the sole aim of carrying out your duty as a reproductive unit of the human race?

BERNARD: (*After a moment's thought.*) No.

ADRIEN: Well then.

Silence. Each of them sunk in reflection at their desks. ADRIEN gets up, goes into the store-room and comes back with a painting wrapped in brown paper. He hands it to BERNARD and kisses him.

Happy birthday, Bernard.

BERNARD: Why now?

ADRIEN: Well it's… Tonight, you see, I've told Léo about this, I just can't make it…

BERNARD: You can't come? (*Pause.*) Can't you even drop in for a minute?

ADRIEN: It's slap bang on the one night I can't.

BERNARD: But how long have you known?

ADRIEN: Known? ... Well, no...

BERNARD: When did Léo tell you about tonight?

ADRIEN: No, that's not the problem...

BERNARD: Yes it is! Did she throw this together at the last minute? There'll be no one there; this is so bloody stupid.

ADRIEN: It's not Léo. She's...it's been...she's been planning all this since January.

BERNARD: And you knew three months ago you wouldn't be free this evening?

ADRIEN: Yes...it's a bit...

BERNARD: (*Stunned.*) Yes, it is...

Silence. BERNARD stares straight ahead.

ADRIEN: Would you rather open it later?

BERNARD: Hmm? No. No, no...

He opens his present. It's a picture of a pretty house surrounded by greenery. BERNARD stares at it unseeingly. ADRIEN pretends not to notice the state BERNARD's in.

ADRIEN: It's 'the happy house'.

BERNARD: (*Absently.*) Yes...true. It looks like it. Eh? It looks like the house.

ADRIEN: It doesn't look like it. It *is* your house. I had it done.

Pause. BERNARD still doesn't surface.

I've got a mate who's a painter... (*Pause.*) He does design as well. (*Pause.*) For theatre, TV...

BERNARD: Oh…

ADRIEN: He works from photos.

BERNARD: Really?

ADRIEN: He came and took one when you weren't in.

BERNARD: (*Staring at the picture.*) It looks abandoned… (*He kisses ADRIEN.*) I really like it.

ADRIEN: It really is the happy house.

BERNARD smiles stiffly.

I don't know what to say about tonight.

BERNARD: No, no…I understand…

ADRIEN: You understand what?

BERNARD: It really doesn't matter…

ADRIEN: Bernard, I'm telling you that…

BERNARD: We spend all day working together…

ADRIEN: That's no excuse for missing your fortieth!

BERNARD: You'd have been bored rigid anyway. We hardly have any friends in common. Just as well, that's why we still get on.

ADRIEN: You're right but that's not why.

BERNARD: (*Dryly.*) Why what?

ADRIEN: You seem to be saying that I'm trying to get out of it. I mean…I didn't decide not to come tonight because I was scared I'd be bored. We're friends… more than friends. It's not because I wouldn't know many people…I'd have loved to be there! I'd have loved it, and I'm really, really sorry to miss it. Do you understand?

BERNARD: I understand that your life is very…well, very… (*He gestures to suggest something very tight.*) So, you're overbooked.

ADRIEN: I'm not overbooked, I just can't do tonight, these things happen, bloody hell!

BERNARD: Bloody hell is right! You haven't got a watch. You haven't got a diary. If a girl so much as leaves her toothbrush at your place you dump her. You're allergic to the slightest suggestion of planning ahead. Every time we try to arrange a holiday together it cocks up precisely because you're incapable of organizing your schedule more than forty-eight hours in advance, and now you're telling me that you knew three months ago that you wouldn't be free to come to my fortieth birthday party because you had a prior engagement that evening! So yes, Adrien, perhaps I am a bit on the touchy side, but forgive me if I'm a little…just a little taken aback.

ADRIEN: You're not taken aback, you're bloody furious.

BERNARD: I'm hurt.

ADRIEN: And I'm hurt that you think I've made up some rubbish story to get out of your party.

BERNARD: Is it a woman? Have you got a…I don't know… a tryst?

ADRIEN: You'd be the first to know.

BERNARD: I'm not asking.

ADRIEN: If it was that I'd have brought her with me.

BERNARD: Brought who?

ADRIEN: No one! If I'd had a 'tryst' I'd have asked Léo if it was okay to bring the lady in question to your party. But there's no...there's no such lady.

BERNARD: But there could have been.

ADRIEN: There could have been but there isn't.

BERNARD: Right... But there could have been.

ADRIEN: Well sure...but there isn't.

BERNARD picks up his briefcase and makes to leave.

BERNARD: I think we deserve to shut up shop a bit early today.

ADRIEN: Where are you going?

BERNARD: Home.

ADRIEN: It's way too early. Léo told me to keep you out of the way till half eight.

BERNARD: Don't worry, I'll stay out till then. (*Holds out his hand.*) See you. And well done!

ADRIEN: Well done you. You did most of it.

BERNARD: (*Coldly.*) Well done both of us. See you.

ADRIEN: Let's go for a swift one! Bernard...

BERNARD: No thanks, I need some... [*fresh air.*]

BERNARD opens the door.

ADRIEN: Are you not taking your present?

BERNARD: Hmm? Oh yes...

He picks up the picture and glances at it as if seeing the house for the first time. Goes towards the door.

ADRIEN: This is so stupid.

BERNARD: What? What's so stupid?

ADRIEN: To be like this on a day like today.

BERNARD: I just can't stand dishonesty.

ADRIEN: What dishonesty?

BERNARD: Look I'm giving you a hard time, it's silly, I mean, we just work together that's all. You can do whatever you like in the evenings obviously...

ADRIEN: Bernard.

BERNARD: No, no, no, you're right and I'm wrong, I can see that. All that cake and candle stuff just isn't your thing...

ADRIEN: Bernard...!

BERNARD: What?

ADRIEN: I'll come round tomorrow, the day after tomorrow and every day for a week! I dream of spending whole nights blowing out candles till I'm sick, with friends who I love, admire and envy. Just tonight I can't!

BERNARD: Fine. And you refuse to say why?

ADRIEN: No I don't! You haven't asked!

BERNARD: So if I asked, you'd tell me?

ADRIEN: Yes.

BERNARD: Well I'm asking.

ADRIEN: All right then; it's the first Thursday of the month and on the first Thursday of every month it's the monthly dinner at my club.

BERNARD: Your what?

ADRIEN: My club…

BERNARD: I see…you only had to say.

ADRIEN: Well I've said.

Pause. ADRIEN lights a cigarette.

BERNARD: (*Amused.*) You're in a club, are you?

ADRIEN: Yeah, yeah, yeah. What's the face for?

BERNARD: …?

ADRIEN: That little smirk… I know exactly what you're thinking.

BERNARD: Do you really? I don't think I'm thinking anything in particular…

ADRIEN: Oh yes you are. You're thinking that under the lean, lone-wolf exterior I'm just like everybody else… Commitment-phobic, but has to have his little, monthly, regulated dose of social intercourse served up for him all neat and tidy…

BERNARD: I'm not thinking that at all…

ADRIEN: You were just then, but now you're already thinking something else, oh yes the tiny brain is whirring round! … Now you're thinking, 'This club thing is all very well but look, their dinner is once a month; my birthday's only once a year, and my fortieth is once in my entire lifetime…!'

BERNARD: Yes, I admit that some such vague idea may have flitted across the back of my mind.

ADRIEN: Well look... All right, I'll explain. This club...it's ridiculous, it's not really a club at all... Well, there are no rules except just this one: anyone who misses the club dinner on the first Thursday in the month, even if it's only once, is automatically expelled. That's the thing.

BERNARD: And that would be a big deal would it, being expelled?

ADRIEN: Would it be a big deal for you to be expelled...I don't know...from your house, or...

BERNARD: Oh right, as important as that...

ADRIEN: These are people I can rely on. And they can rely on me. When I was really low, really desperate, they all did a little something for me... Nothing huge. The odd little gesture of humanity...

BERNARD: Did any of them offer you a job?

ADRIEN: No, you did that.

BERNARD: Yes, that's rather what I... [*That's what I thought.*]

ADRIEN: Bernard, it's not written down in the friendship rule-book that it has to come to an end if either party fails to attend the other's birthday party.

BERNARD: Oh no?

ADRIEN: No.

BERNARD: So what is in the friendship rule-book then?

ADRIEN: There isn't one. That's what's so lovely about it. When you decide to go into partnership there are

papers to sign; when you decide to get married there
are papers to sign; when you decide to be friends...well
that's just it, you don't decide...it's just something that
happens...it's like getting a present.

BERNARD: And this is why you'd rather go and have dinner
with these guys than...

ADRIEN: It's not a question of 'rather'. If I miss this dinner
I'm out, that's all.

Pause. BERNARD thinks.

BERNARD: And what makes you so sure you're not going
to terminally offend me? Okay so there's no rule-book
for friends but there are guidelines...they may not be
written down and perhaps, perhaps we don't talk about
them, but they're there!

ADRIEN: Who was it who said that a friend is someone you
can phone in the middle of the night and say, 'I've just
killed a man,' and he'll say, 'Okay, where's the body?'

BERNARD: What's that got to do with anything?

ADRIEN: Why are you so prickly about this? Why not put
yourself in my place for a second?

BERNARD: Prickly?

ADRIEN: You're not even trying to understand.

BERNARD: So explain!

ADRIEN: Yes but no that's just it! The guy who calls
his mate in the middle of the night doesn't have to
explain...

BERNARD: Right, fine but this isn't the middle of the night!
This is such sophistical shit!

ADRIEN: It's what?

BERNARD: Nothing. It's broad daylight, that's all.
Everything's very clear... Oh, you turn everything
round! You're the one sneaking off on my fortieth
birthday and I'm the Judas!

ADRIEN: I'm not sneaking off; I don't have any choice.

BERNARD: What kind of club is this? Some sort of cult?

ADRIEN: It's not a cult. It's not...it's not even...it's nothing,
it's a connection. Yeah, that's it. Something that
connects me...keeps me connected, stops me... [*floating
away.*]

BERNARD: What about us? We don't have a connection?

ADRIEN: Yes, Bernard, of course we have.

BERNARD: But since I'm not as demanding as your 'club'...

ADRIEN: You're a million times more demanding. We're
both a million times more demanding towards each
other than any club to its members. But the fact is that
this club does demand just the one thing and that is that
we all meet up once a month...

BERNARD: ...on the first Thursday of the month. What
is it with this club anyway. How come you've never
mentioned it?

ADRIEN: Because...You know, it's not even all that...
[*terribly important.*]

BERNARD: Oh yes it is! Why have you never mentioned it
to me?

ADRIEN: I don't know...I don't tell you... [*everything.*]

BERNARD: Ah but you do. You do tell me everything.

ADRIEN: Would you rather I didn't?

BERNARD: It's not a question of what I'd rather. I'm simply saying that you're not all that terribly...

ADRIEN: Discreet?

BERNARD: You're not the kind of person who keeps hidden secrets. Not with me. What is this club? What sort of club is it?

ADRIEN: It's a club.

BERNARD: What does that mean, it's a club? A sports club? Christmas club? Kennel club? Do you get your stamp collections out and do swapsies?

ADRIEN: Not as far as I know...

BERNARD: So what is it? Movers and shakers?

ADRIEN: When I first joined, I was out of work and I'd just got divorced...so, no, not really.

BERNARD: So it's a kind of association...a sort of self-help thing for...

ADRIEN: For saddos?

BERNARD: Give over. There are groups like that, guys who used to be long-term unemployed and they get together to help people look for work.

ADRIEN: There isn't a set aim, as such... The people are... They're... Well there's your dentist, for example... We don't really talk about work... It's just...you know...

BERNARD: My dentist? Doctor Boulanger's a member?

ADRIEN nods.

What's he like?

ADRIEN: Well he's…well you know him.

BERNARD: I don't know him. He's been telling me the same three anecdotes every six months for fifteen years while he pokes about in my mouth…

ADRIEN: Exactly… I mean, he steers clear of our mouths but I'm sure he only knows three anecdotes, you're right about that…

BERNARD: And has it got a name, this club?

ADRIEN: The painter who did your picture, he's a member too actually…

BERNARD: Oh…

Pause. BERNARD stares blankly.

ADRIEN: Bernard…?

BERNARD: Hmm?

ADRIEN: All right?

BERNARD: (*Staring straight ahead.*) Has it got a name?

ADRIEN: Not really, no…

BERNARD: It's not… Is it a lodge? Are you a mason?

ADRIEN: No, no.

BERNARD: Is it a sort of Rotary thing, Oddfellows… Buffalos?

ADRIEN: No, it's nothing… Look… It's not even serious really… We're called The Hedgehogs…it's pathetic…

BERNARD: And my birthday is even more pathetic, is it?

ADRIEN: Socially, it's a pathetic club. Look…

BERNARD: The Hedgehogs, eh?

ADRIEN nods. Pause.

But with the pricks on the inside?

ADRIEN smiles wearily.

Have you got, like a handshake, or a sign, you know, to identify each other... A little badge or something?

ADRIEN: There's a sort of... (*Gestures vaguely.*)

BERNARD: Collar? Ruff? False beard?

ADRIEN: ...a sort of tie. It's a joke really...

BERNARD: Is that it?

ADRIEN: You gave me this one.

BERNARD: Can I see it? This tie...

ADRIEN: I haven't got it on me.

BERNARD: What'll you do about tonight?

ADRIEN: I've told you. It's no big thing. You don't have to wear it.

BERNARD: And...can anyone join? ... What? Sorry, am I boring you?

ADRIEN: No...I don't know what you've got into your head here...it's just a little...

BERNARD: It's not just a little anything, it's a 'connection'. You just said that if you were kicked out it'd be like me being dumped by my wife...the mother of my children...and now the bloody thing barely exists. So if it barely exists you can come tonight and we'll forget all about it.

ADRIEN: It does exist. Just because it exists doesn't necessarily make it interesting.

BERNARD: Oh yes it does! It's weird...it's... I don't know... I just can't see you in a club somehow... To me the whole club thing is more...it's more a kind of old gents, leather armchairs, brandy and soda, cigarish, Jeevesy kind of thing. 'Just off to my club, old boy.'

ADRIEN: It's the word. 'Club'... Let's say it's a group of guys who get together on a regular basis...

BERNARD: Ah yes, but it's not that, is it? If you get expelled for missing one dinner then it's not...it's...well, it's exclusive, isn't it? You can be excluded. And it's not open-door, I suppose, you can't just walk up and join... Can you?

ADRIEN: You join...

BERNARD: Take me, say if I wanted to join...

ADRIEN: Well why not...?

BERNARD: How did you come to join?

ADRIEN: A friend of a friend put me forward.

BERNARD: Anyone I know?

ADRIEN: I don't think so, no. No.

BERNARD: And what do you do once you're in?

ADRIEN: Nothing!

BERNARD: I mean, can you nominate other people?

ADRIEN: You have to be a member for a certain period of time...three years I think it is...and after that you can put forward one person per year for membership.

BERNARD: Have you put anyone forward yet at all?

ADRIEN: No.

Pause. ADRIEN looks impatient.

BERNARD: Still an hour to go.

ADRIEN: Hmm?

BERNARD: Léo told you to keep me away until half eight.

ADRIEN: D'you fancy a drink?

BERNARD: We've still to drink to that sacred bond which unites us!

ADRIEN: Irony?

BERNARD fills their glasses.

BERNARD: To our success.

ADRIEN: And a very happy birthday.

BERNARD: Well it's started brilliantly. No, I mean it!

They drink. Long silence.

So look, these Hedgehogs of yours...

ADRIEN grimaces.

What? ... What? Is it a banned subject?

ADRIEN: It's not banned it's just boring.

BERNARD: Do I know any others? Your mate on the planning committee, you know, is he one?

ADRIEN: Who? ... No.

BERNARD: So you and my dentist are the only two Hedgehogs I know?

ADRIEN sighs half-way between laughter and exasperation.

ADRIEN: All right, look, no. You know Roly as well.

BERNARD: Roly?

ADRIEN: Roland.

BERNARD: Who's Roland?

ADRIEN: Your pal Chicamour.

Pause. BERNARD staggers under the blow.

BERNARD: (*Stunned.*) Of course... (*Pause.*) Chicamour...of course... Roly?

ADRIEN: We all have a sort of nickname.

BERNARD: Yours being...?

ADRIEN: Addy. Adrien. Addy...

BERNARD: My dentist?

ADRIEN: Chippy.

BERNARD: Isn't he called Bruno?

ADRIEN: Yes, but there's already a Brian we call Brysy, so...

BERNARD: Where do you get Chippy?

ADRIEN: It's from Chipolata. He made it up himself. Because of his...

BERNARD: Yes, quite. (*Pause. BERNARD gets up like a sleepwalker.*) Good, fine...

He takes up his painting and makes to leave. Crushed. ADRIEN glances at his watch.

ADRIEN: It's too early...

BERNARD: (*Flat.*) I'm going for a little walk... (*He opens the door.*)

ADRIEN: Bernard...

BERNARD exits.

BERNARD: (*Off.*) Give my regards to Roly...

ADRIEN doesn't move for a few moments, lost in thought. Then he gets up and undoes his tie. He takes another tie from his pocket. He unrolls it and carefully ties it as the light slowly fades.

Scene 2

Morning. The office is deserted. ADRIEN enters looking drawn. He's had little or no sleep. He puts his motorbike helmet down in a corner. He picks up the phone. At the same time, his mobile rings. He hangs up the phone and answers the mobile.

ADRIEN: Yes? ... Léo, yes, I was just going to call you. Is he back? ... No, he's not here... (*Trying to calm her down.*) Hang on now, Léo, try and... Steady... I know but... Léo, I've told you already, if something bad's happened to someone... No, Léo, that's what I'm saying! Someone would have called you, he had ID on him, didn't he... Yes but even so... Have you tried his mobile? ... Well, try again, you never know... Okay, okay, you try his mobile now, I'll be right here, I'm not going anywhere... (*Soothingly.*) I'm sure of it... Yes...

He hangs up. Pause. The muffled ring of a mobile is heard. ADRIEN gets up and hunts around... The ringing is coming from the bathroom. ADRIEN rushes over and flings the door open. BERNARD's legs tumble out; he's unconscious. We can't see the rest of his body but we assume he's laid out in the toilet. ADRIEN seizes BERNARD's mobile and answers it.

Léo, it's me! Adrien!… He's here… I'll call you back… All right all right, hang on… I won't hang up just hold on…

He puts down the mobile ands bends over BERNARD's body, which is still out of sight.

(*From off.*) Bernard? Bernard, can you hear me?

BERNARD groans weakly.

Bernard, try and open your eyes… Can you hear me? … Bernard! Are you hurt? … You have to wake up, Bernard…

We hear a series of increasingly violent slaps, each one followed by increasingly distinct groans.

BERNARD: (*Off, very drowsy.*) Oww… Get off…!

ADRIEN: Open your eyes! Come on, open up… There we are!

ADRIEN helps BERNARD up and picks up the mobile while supporting him. BERNARD is in the same clothes as the night before but very crumpled.

(*On phone.*) Léo? Did you hear him? … No, he's fine, I think he's fine… He's very… Eh? … Well, to be honest, he's overdone it a bit… I can smell it, that's why… No I don't think so… I really don't think a stomach pump will be… Well, because he's taken care of it himself… Yes, all over the shop… Don't worry… (*To BERNARD.*) Eyes! Open! (*On phone.*) No, not at the moment… I can't put him on just now, Léo, he's not well… He's fine it's just that he's really not well! … No that's a really terrible idea… I'm not just looking out for my mate, Léo, this is not a good time for you to pop over…

BERNARD is holding his skull to stop it exploding.

He'll call you back… He's fine, he's alive, he's standing on his own two feet…

BERNARD collapses slowly like a heap of dirty washing.

Everything's fine…we'll call you right back…

ADRIEN hangs up. Long silence. BERNARD straightens up with difficulty. He looks at ADRIEN. The ghost of a smile plays on his lips. ADRIEN gets coffee and brings it over to where BERNARD has slumped in his chair. BERNARD takes a sip and looks at ADRIEN like a little boy.

BERNARD: (*Sheepishly.*) Sugar?

ADRIEN puts the sugar down next to BERNARD's cup. Before drinking, BERNARD clinks cups with ADRIEN. They drink in silence.

ADRIEN: You should call her back.

Pause.

BERNARD: Hmm?

ADRIEN: What?

BERNARD: (*Glancing at his wrist.*) Someone's nicked my watch… Oh no, I gave it to somebody… I swapped it. For this!

He takes out a little mechanical toy which sniggers and turns somersaults.

Isn't it fab?

He tries to turn it off but the thing keeps sniggering. Eventually, he smashes it against the desk to shut it up.

It's fab but it doesn't tell the time... It was the Rolex I got for our tenth anniversary... D'you think I've been had?

The toy gives one last little snigger before conking out completely. BERNARD gets up and walks robotically to the toilet. He disappears inside. We hear him throwing up and then copiously rinsing his mouth out. He comes back bare-chested with a towel in his hand.

What about you? ... Good night?

ADRIEN: Me... Léo called me the first time around half nine. She thought you were still with me. After that we phoned each other every fifteen minutes. I left my dinner early and got to your place around eleven. We waited up all night for you. About four-ish I went to the police, to see if... Then I went back to yours and that was about it. I have to say, I have spent evenings with more... So, all things considered, it was a totally shit night. Thanks for asking.

Pause.

BERNARD: I nipped into the station bar for a quick one... You know?

ADRIEN: No.

BERNARD: Bugger! Bugger, bugger, bugger!

ADRIEN: What?

BERNARD: Your present. I've left it somewhere. I've lost your painting!

ADRIEN: Call the bar. They're bound to have kept it.

BERNARD: No, no! I know I had it when I left there...
So after that... Where can I have left it? ... My little
house...

*The phone rings like a bradawl in BERNARD's skull. He
signals ADRIEN to answer it.*

ADRIEN: Hello...Yes, he's right here...

*He holds the phone out to BERNARD, indicating that it's
Léo. Pause. BERNARD hesitates. ADRIEN keeps his arm
held out, then pretends he's going to hang up. BERNARD
takes the receiver.*

BERNARD: Hi there? ... Well, Adrien's told you, I'm not in
peak form but I'm okay... I've lost my watch... I don't
know. I honestly don't know... No, there's a lot to do
here, I'll try not to be too late... What did people say?
... Yeah, sure... What about presents, did they leave
them there? ... Are there lots? ... (*To ADRIEN.*) That's it,
of course! Your picture! (*Into phone.*) Adrien gave me a
really lovely picture of our house, our little cottage...I
thought I'd lost it last night but now... (*To ADRIEN
without covering the receiver.*) I left it at Nadia's...your little
friend, you know...that slapper-cum-tart who hangs
around the sports bar... (*Into phone.*) Eh? ... Nothing, I
left the picture at some girl's... Just a girl, ask Adrien, he
knows her better than I do... Yes, at her place, she's got
a pretty grubby bed-sit near where the new post office
is... Well, obviously! Darling, she's a whore! You don't
think I'd pay a whore for a nice little chat! I haven't
sunk that far! ... A whore, with a whore's tits, a whore's
arse and a dirty whore's tongue. Well no, she's quite
well-spoken actually, but a whore's mouth, you know,
she could suck a tennis ball through a hose-pipe...
Hello? ... Hello? ...

A pause. Léo has hung up. BERNARD passes the receiver to ADRIEN who hangs up. It rings instantly. ADRIEN answers.

ADRIEN: Hello... Speaking... Thank you... (*To BERNARD.*) It's Legrand. (*Into phone.*) Yes, hello, how are you, Mr Legrand? ...Jacques... How are you, Jacques? ... Absolutely! Absolutely delighted! A little...in awe when we think about the sheer magnitude of the project but... Lunch? Today? Um, today...

BERNARD tries to take the phone. ADRIEN keeps a grip on it.

Yes, fine... Not at all... Great, see you then... (*He hangs up.*) We're having lunch with him and some girl from the Mayor's office.

BERNARD: Could you... Could you lend me a shirt and tie?

ADRIEN: Is this all connected?

BERNARD: What?

ADRIEN gets out a shirt which is identical to the one he's wearing and gives it to BERNARD.

ADRIEN: Is this all connected with...it is, isn't it?

BERNARD: I don't understand.

ADRIEN: Is there a connection...a causal connection between what happened with us last night and this...this absolutely titanic cock-up?

BERNARD: What happened with us last night? ...What did happen?

ADRIEN: Yes, exactly, what did happen?

BERNARD: Perhaps I'd better phone her back...

ADRIEN: And say what...?

BERNARD: I don't know...that...

ADRIEN: That whores' tits leave you cold and being sucked through a hose isn't really your cup of tea after all and so, well, there you go, oops!

Pause. BERNARD rubs his temples.

Well?

BERNARD: I'll tell her it was a joke...an idiotic bet with you...you know... I'd bet you I could say the word 'whore' five times to the next person who rang up... No? ... Help!

ADRIEN: Get dressed. Get into that nice big car of yours, zoom straight home and beg her on your knees till she forgives you.

BERNARD: Do you think she might?

ADRIEN: If you get going right now.

BERNARD: Why?

ADRIEN: Because Léo's a...

BERNARD: A sucker!

ADRIEN: That's not exactly what I was going to say...

BERNARD: Léo's an 'amazing woman'! Our relationship is a shining example to all of you... In other words: Léo's a sucker, I'm a loser, and all we're good for is banging away like battery hens and turning out lots more little losers and suckers!

ADRIEN: 'Banging away like battery hens...'??

BERNARD: Did you hear what I've just done to my wife? … And you claim… You have the royal, bloody nerve to claim that she'll let me off scot-free if I just spend a moment or two down on my knees on the nice comfy carpet?

ADRIEN: I think you're grown-ups. You're both grown-ups. You're a grown-up couple.

BERNARD: So what about you?

ADRIEN: What about me?

BERNARD: You've just given me some advice. Why don't you follow it yourself?

ADRIEN: You want me to beg your wife to forgive you?

BERNARD: Oh no, you should be begging me!

ADRIEN: Aha!

BERNARD: You should be asking me to forgive you…!

ADRIEN: Bingo! It is connected! It's all my fault!

BERNARD: Ah, but no! You won't catch Adrien begging anyone! No chance! And don't you go thinking that you've made some kind of connection with Adrien…!

ADRIEN: Who are you talking to?

BERNARD: …Adrien doesn't do connections!

ADRIEN: Who's he talking to?

BERNARD: Oh yes, that's right.

ADRIEN: What are you on about? What is this performance?

BERNARD: Oh no, Adrien only acknowledges the one connection…

ADRIEN: Hello! I'm Adrien. I'm over here if you fancy a chat…

BERNARD: No, he won't listen! You see?

ADRIEN: I'm going for a coffee…

BERNARD: The only connection acknowledged by this bloody, little…

He can't find an epithet sufficiently contemptuous; ADRIEN waits by the door to hear the rest.

…the only one, is a club. And do you know why?

ADRIEN: No.

BERNARD: (*To ADRIEN.*) No?

ADRIEN: No…

BERNARD: Well Adrien knows…oh yes, he knows very well but he won't say. Shall I tell you why? … The reason Adrien hasn't got a wife or any friends. The reason all he's got in his life is a club which chucks you out if you miss the monthly Thursday evening dinner is…

Pause. BERNARD has got a bit tangled up in his reasoning.

ADRIEN: The reason is…?

BERNARD: You know bloody well what I mean!

Pause. ADRIEN doesn't seem to get it.

That is the reason! Because they chuck you out if you miss the fucking dinner! That's it, you're out! No point pleading with them, that's just the way it is, it's written down in black and white, that's the rule. In fact, it's the only rule! So it's really simple, and everything else, all the stuff like friendship, love, feelings, relationships, responsibilities... Fuck the lot of it! Who needs it? It's only for the losers and the suckers, all that!

Pause. BERNARD puts on the shirt that ADRIEN has lent him.

ADRIEN: You didn't go to Nadia's... All this lunatic... Don't tell me you've done all this to teach me some kind of lesson? ... Is that it? ... You do realise that it's not me who's going to be most affected by this...shambles? I mean...you're the one who's going to suffer most, followed by Léo, and the girls, and a long, long way after that, maybe me, just a little...

Pause. BERNARD thinking it over.

You'll have to help me out here... What's the problem? Exactly? You're hurt. Why are you hurt?

BERNARD: Just put my mind at rest, would you? I hope they didn't expel you last night because you had to 'cut short' the dinner?

ADRIEN: Could you just set out in plain words what it is that's hurt you?

BERNARD: Why have you never suggested it to me?

ADRIEN: Suggested what?

BERNARD: Your club. Me joining your club.

ADRIEN: I don't think...I didn't think you'd particularly fancy having dinner with Chicamour once a month.

BERNARD: Yes, but why?

ADRIEN: Because I don't reckon you like him very much.

BERNARD: Do you like him? Do you respect him?

ADRIEN: Who, Chicamour?

BERNARD: Roly.

ADRIEN: Hmm… No. I can't honestly say I respect Roly all that much.

BERNARD: So why then? Why you and not me?

ADRIEN: You and not me what?

BERNARD: You've just told me that the reason I wouldn't want to be in the club is because I don't like one of the members, but now you don't like him either so…so…so explain it to me!

ADRIEN: No, you explain this! Explain how you can rabbit on about Chicamour and some crappy club when your wife…Have you any idea at all what she's been going through since yesterday evening?

BERNARD: I want to join this club.

ADRIEN: Why?

BERNARD: Why not?

ADRIEN: There's got to be a way to…I don't know…to sort this mess out…to fix it… We're friends… You're my friend, and Léo, Léo's a friend now too, she really is… You've… [*said some terrible things to her.*] She… [*must be shattered.*] Time's ticking away… Bernard, I'm sure we can make this all right… We'll cancel lunch with Legrand… I'll call Léo… What is it?

BERNARD: What made you want to join?

ADRIEN: Bernard. You're not mad. I know you're not. Stop this!

BERNARD: What would I need that I haven't got?

ADRIEN: Meaning?

BERNARD: What would I need to be a Hedgehog?

ADRIEN: Nothing!

BERNARD: You're dodging the issue! I tell you I want to join and you ask me why; so I ask you why you wanted to join and you refuse to say…

ADRIEN: I didn't want to join!

BERNARD: Oh, come on. You are here in this room because you entered it, because you *wanted* to enter it, and when you leave it, it'll be because you *want* to…and if I were to smack you in the mouth right now, it'd be because I *want* to!

ADRIEN: If that's how you want it, bring it on, let's get it over with…

BERNARD: Why did you join this club?

ADRIEN: I joined by osmosis.

BERNARD: Osmosis?!

ADRIEN: Yes. Bernard, you've got friends, and those friends form groups, or gangs, or whatever you want to call it… You don't join, as such, you're just in! It's the same thing! We call it The Hedgehogs but it doesn't mean anything. It's a group of friends.

BERNARD: And I'm not in it. I'm not included in your friends.

ADRIEN: You are my friend. You're just not in this…

BERNARD: This world.

ADRIEN: This particular group! And you've got a certain circle of friends that I'm not in. You said yourself that I'd be bored at your party because I wouldn't have known many people.

BERNARD: I only said that to…so you wouldn't feel guilty at missing the fortieth birthday of your business partner and…

ADRIEN: And friend.

BERNARD: You didn't just wake up one morning as a member of the CLUB!

ADRIEN: Yes I did. I did virtually…

BERNARD: (*Calmer tone, changing tack.*) No, hang on, hang on now, I simply want to understand… It's not a matter of… I don't give a toss about the club, as such… That's not the point. It's just… It's not a secret society is it? I mean, you can talk about it can you? I mean I don't know…

ADRIEN: I can talk about it. It's just, I can't help thinking there are more urgent things to sort out…

BERNARD: Well that's for me to judge…

ADRIEN looks doubtful, causing BERNARD's rage to reignite.

Yes it is! What more urgent things? It was pretty urgent to get to your do last night, wasn't it?

ADRIEN: That's over now!

BERNARD: It's not over! I can't get over it!

ADRIEN: Bernard. Bernard! I had dinner… It's a bunch of mates. I had dinner with a bunch of mates.

BERNARD: Oh no you don't! Stop that! You're playing it down now! When I talk to you about my wife I don't call her 'some bird' do I? No, I say 'my wife'.

ADRIEN: Your wife, that's right, your wife!

BERNARD: It wasn't 'a bunch of mates' yesterday, was it? Oh no, it was 'The Monthly Dinner At My Club'.

ADRIEN: So what?

BERNARD: (*Returning to his interrogation.*) When you joined this club, did you or did you not already know all the other members?

ADRIEN: Some.

BERNARD: What's the form? Did someone recommend you? Did someone propose you or put your name forward or something or what?

ADRIEN: I told you yesterday…

BERNARD: Yes or no? Adrien, what's the problem here? Are you scared I'm going to ask you to propose me? Is that it?

ADRIEN: For goodness' sake…you're freaking me out here…

BERNARD: All I'm asking…it's perfectly straightforward… what's the…just what do you have to do to join?

ADRIEN: You have to be a man.

BERNARD: I see…and you just get together and decide that, do you? This guy's a man; this guy, don't think so…

ADRIEN: No, not a man… A man. The club's men only… not mixed.

BERNARD: Is that it?

ADRIEN: That's it… That's the only condition. It's what they call a necessary condition…not sufficient, but necessary…

BERNARD: And I'm not sufficient?

ADRIEN: You're a pain in the arse!

BERNARD: So what about the sufficient conditions?

ADRIEN: There aren't any. That's the only condition.

BERNARD: But you've just said it's only a necessary condition.

ADRIEN: That's right. Bernard…

BERNARD: So what other conditions are there? Other requirements?

ADRIEN: I don't know. Honestly, I don't know…

BERNARD: But there are some, right? You agree there must be some?

ADRIEN: There must be…but it's…

BERNARD: It's…?

ADRIEN: It's…I don't know…

BERNARD: So you're saying you were chosen…you were picked out according to certain criteria that you know absolutely nothing about? Is that what you're saying?

ADRIEN stares at BERNARD as if he's completely mad. BERNARD looks back.

ADRIEN: There aren't any criteria.

BERNARD: So any man, any male whatsoever, is eligible to join?

ADRIEN: Yes, in principle.

BERNARD: In principle?

ADRIEN: That's right.

BERNARD: But as a matter of actual fact, certain men are members, and certain others not.

ADRIEN: Well it's a club. Obviously there has to be a…

BERNARD: A barrier.

ADRIEN: A boundary.

BERNARD: Bollocks! Barrier. Boundary.

ADRIEN: Affinities.

BERNARD: So you have affinities with my dentist? And you and me? We don't?

ADRIEN: All right. There are requirements. But they aren't…it's more…

BERNARD: Unwritten?

ADRIEN: Maybe…yes…unwritten, that's right.

BERNARD: So what is it that's unwritten?

ADRIEN: Like you just said.

BERNARD: No… You're telling me that there are, in fact, entrance requirements for your club but that they're unwritten, implicit criteria…they're not laid out, as such…so, what I'm saying is…that's easy enough! … Let's lay them out. (*Silence.*) Just what do these unwritten requirements involve? Exactly what are the implications of these implicit criteria? (*Silence.*) Adrien, I know… I understand that you're concerned, you're worried about my relationship with my wife. And I'm grateful. But look, you and I have a relationship going here as well, we're linked together, partners in crime, we're supposed to work together, our livelihood depends on this bond between us…

ADRIEN: What bond? … You keep going on about us being linked, about our 'relationship' about our 'bond'. Partners in crime? What did we do?

BERNARD: No, it's just…it's a spontaneous thing. You can't explain it.

ADRIEN: Oh right, I see, you can't explain it.

BERNARD: It just…is. You said it yourself. There's no rules, no papers to sign, it's like getting a present! … Adrien, I'm trying to salvage something here…

ADRIEN: I'm the one who's trying to salvage… What are you trying to salvage? You're just stamping your little foot and smashing everything up like a spoiled little brat.

BERNARD: I'm trying…I am trying to understand why you don't consider me worthy to be part of something which has such paramount importance in your life. Not even worthy to know it exists! It's as if I hadn't told you I was married!

ADRIEN: Well yes, but…no, hang on! Comparing your marriage to…that's actually not a bad point… It's like saying that your relationship…you and Léo are the only two members of a sort of ultra-exclusive club! You see? Yes, that's exactly it. You chose each other according to certain unwritten entrance requirements, and that was it, lock the door... Private club. Members only!

BERNARD: And so our door is locked, is it? To you, for example?

ADRIEN: No, of course your house is open, wide open, in you come! Roll up and gasp in admiration at the perfect couple and their three model kids... Roll up and marvel at our happiness – it's so smooth, it's so flawless and shiny it's like sodding stainless steel...

BERNARD: Oh, yes, absolutely, that's it. Our hospitality is a cunning scheme to shove our smug, self-satisfied, perfect life in your face. And what about you? What a model of openness and generosity you are with your secrets and your neatly ordered cupboards and oh, look at my mistresses, my business partner, my dry-cleaning, and my club, my men only club, my men-with-big-hairy-swinging-bollocks only club.

ADRIEN: Things really aren't that simple...

BERNARD: Things are simple! They just need to be spelled out. After five years I find out that you belong to some sort of brotherhood from which you have rigorously excluded me. And there's me thinking all this time that I was like a kind of brother to you myself.

ADRIEN: I haven't excluded you from anything!

BERNARD: You took the decision for me that I wouldn't fit in.

ADRIEN: And that's what you're accusing me of?

BERNARD: I'm accusing you... I'm accusing you of ducking the issue.

ADRIEN: What issue?

BERNARD: You're being evasive. You're dodging the dooberry...

ADRIEN: Okay, okay... Ask me what you want to ask. Give me a straight question and I'll try and give you a straight answer. No ducking.

BERNARD: Fine.

ADRIEN: Go on then.

BERNARD: Right... Okay... What I want... I'd like... I'm putting myself forward for membership... I wish to be a Hedgehog. (*Silence.*) Well?

ADRIEN: Well what? I'm still waiting for a question.

BERNARD: Well – question mark – yes or no, are you prepared to propose me for membership of the club?

Silence. The phone rings. ADRIEN picks up.

ADRIEN: Hello... Hello darling, how are you? Yes, your Daddy's here. I'll just put him on... What? ... Why don't you want to marry me anymore? I've been waiting for you, you know... There's a lot of very unhappy girls out there because I've told them I can't marry them because of you... Robinson? Who's Robinson? In your class, is he? ... I don't make you laugh? ... Oh, right, I see... Yeah, not bad. Can he blow square ones? ... No, I can't either but then I'm not a champion bubble-gum blower like he is. I just think it's a bit odd that a bubble-gum champion can't even blow square bubbles... Well okay, you ask him and we'll see... I'm not sure it's all that serious, this Robinson thing... All right, sweetheart, here's your Daddy... (*Holds the phone out to BERNARD.*)

BERNARD: Hello, poppet... No school? ... Oh dear, oh dear. Well I hope the cake was nice at least? ... I just couldn't, I'll tell you all about it when I get home... Is Mummy there? ... What? ... I don't know, I don't think so... (*To ADRIEN.*) Do they have the death penalty in Japan?

ADRIEN: Hara-kiri?

BERNARD: Why are you asking, sweetie? ... What are you worried about? ... And why is your friend Chloe going to Japan? ... Well her Daddy's very lucky to get a job there, it's a lovely country, and so's she... But, sweetheart, you have to do something really, really naughty to be put to death... Well maybe she has, but not as bad as that... I don't know, kill a lot of people, or kill a child, darling, we'll talk about it this evening. Are you sure Mummy isn't there? ... Well can I speak to her then? ... Oh. She definitely said that, did she? She doesn't want to talk to me? ... Why are you crying? ... No, sweetheart, no, nobody's going to kill you! ... No! ... Nobody goes around killing children, well not usually. I was just saying you'd have to slaughter piles of them to get your head chopped off ... 'Guillotine', darling, not 'gelatin'... Not in France, you know they don't cut heads off in France anymore, you've asked me that a thousand times... Everything's all right, poppet... No... No, darling... I know you want to but no... Because you can't eat sweets when you've had a tummy ache the night before! ... Because it's a stupid thing to do! ... Well I'm sorry but it's still no... You can break the phone if you like but it's not the phone's fault, is it? ... Listen now, I'm going to hang up, but I promise I'll bring you a little surprise tonight when I get home... It's a surprise... If I tell you what it is it won't be a surprise will it? … If I tell you now I can't give it you this evening… Because it's…it's no… I've got to go… No, darling, when I say no I mean no! … NO! … (*Counts down very fast.*) Five, four, three, two, one, kiss kiss! …(*He hangs up. Long silence.*) Well?

ADRIEN: What?

BERNARD: The club, is it yes or no?

ADRIEN: It's no.

Blackout.

Scene 3

The work-tables are no longer face-to-face. They are placed in a line downstage, facing out front, as far from each other as possible. It is evening. BERNARD and ADRIEN are working in silence, each by the light of his own lamp, forming two circles of illumination in the gloom. They sit in such a way that they have virtually turned their backs on each other. Silence.

BERNARD: Did you call back about the Renaudin permit?

ADRIEN: Haven't had time…

A silence. ADRIEN tries to light a cigarette with a malfunctioning lighter.

Got a light?

BERNARD: Here…

BERNARD throws him a box of matches, ADRIEN drops it. He picks it up and lights his cigarette.

ADRIEN: Thanks…

Silence. They keep working.

BERNARD: Are those menthols?

ADRIEN: Want one?

BERNARD: Yeah, thanks.

ADRIEN gets up and offers the packet to BERNARD who takes a cigarette. ADRIEN goes back to his place.

Have you got the matches?

ADRIEN throws the box to BERNARD who drops it... They smoke in silence. BERNARD looks at his watch. ADRIEN seems absorbed in his work. BERNARD puts out his cigarette.

Don't know how you can smoke those...

ADRIEN shrugs imperceptibly. BERNARD gets up.

Right. It's about that time...

ADRIEN doesn't even look up from his table. BERNARD gets a tie out of his briefcase and starts to do it up. It is a Hedgehog club tie. BERNARD goes into the bathroom, whistling. ADRIEN stubs his cigarette out, takes another and goes to get the matches from BERNARD's table. He goes back to his place and sits down. BERNARD comes back in with his tie done up and an air of self-satisfaction.

Right... Better be going, hadn't we? ... Don't want to be late my first time... (*He straightens the knot of his tie and shows it to ADRIEN.*) That okay?

ADRIEN glances up a moment, nods vaguely and goes back to his work.

Is there time for a swift one before?

ADRIEN mutters something indistinctly.

Eh?

ADRIEN: Got to finish this off...

BERNARD: Right... Well, okay then, I'll go on ahead and see you there...

ADRIEN: Hmm...

BERNARD: Right... (*He turns his lamp off and makes to go.*) Well, see you soon...

ADRIEN: Yup. Right...

BERNARD hesitates at the door then exits. ADRIEN straightens and sighs out a lungful of smoke. A pause. BERNARD comes back.

BERNARD: It'd be nicer if we arrived together.

ADRIEN: I told you, I've got to finish this.

BERNARD: You can finish it tomorrow.

ADRIEN: I've got to send it all off first thing tomorrow morning.

BERNARD: The whole file?

ADRIEN: The lot.

BERNARD: That's got to be three hours' work...

ADRIEN: That's why.

BERNARD: You're not going to finish that now.

ADRIEN: I promised Legrand I'd send the whole lot over to him by ten tomorrow morning.

BERNARD: We can come back here and finish it together after the dinner if you like.

ADRIEN: I don't think that'd be a good idea.

BERNARD: Or I tell you what, we'll clock in at seven tomorrow morning and...

ADRIEN: I'm going to finish it off now.

Silence. BERNARD stands stock-still. He glances at his watch. ADRIEN keeps working.

BERNARD: What day is it, Adrien?

ADRIEN: Thursday.

BERNARD: And the date?

ADRIEN: It's, uh, the fourth, is it? ...

BERNARD: Which means? (*Pause.*) Adrien, is it or is it not the first Thursday of the month?

ADRIEN: It is.

BERNARD: So stop right now, put that down and let's go.

A silence. ADRIEN looks up at BERNARD.

ADRIEN: You're going to be late.

BERNARD: What's going on?

ADRIEN: What's going on is, there's a job to finish and I can't go to the dinner.

BERNARD: You can't?

ADRIEN: No...

BERNARD: So this is it...

ADRIEN: ...I'm sorry but...

BERNARD: ...this is your little revenge? Your sneaky little scheme... What are you sorry about!?

ADRIEN: Well...this. Everything.

BERNARD: You're not sorry at all, you're loving it. Two weeks you've been sitting there scheming away quietly... You are so petty!

ADRIEN: Bernard, I really don't want to argue... I'm resigning from the club by not turning up tonight, it's no big deal.

BERNARD: Not turning up tonight...not turning up on the night of my official inauguration as a Hedgehog! On the very night I finally earn my spines!

ADRIEN: I've not spent two weeks scheming, this isn't revenge. There's no need to be paranoid, it's got nothing to do with you.

BERNARD: Oh no?

ADRIEN: No.

BERNARD: Well that's a relief. Good, good, fine fine fine... So... Let's say, for example, I don't know, say I'm on a bus; sitting there comfortably reading the paper, and some smelly old tramp comes and sits beside me; and I get up, gagging and holding my nose and head off up the other end of the bus. Would you say he was being paranoid if he thought it might possibly have something to do with him? ... Or say in South Africa, if a black guy's having his lunch in a restaurant and this big fat Boer at the next table jumps up and takes off out of there, screaming about the good old days...

ADRIEN: Yeah, thanks. You can leave the metaphors. I get it.

BERNARD: And do you also get that if you don't change your mind right this minute, the practice, our little business here, the whole thing is over…

ADRIEN: No. I don't get that because I don't really think…

BERNARD: You don't? … For three whole months you refused to propose me for membership of this club. At the time, I let it go, I said to myself that perhaps you were doing it for the sake of our relationship, perhaps you were concerned to re-establish a sort of balance between our work and our private lives which I might possibly have infringed upon… And since then, it so happened that I fell in with another Hedgehog who ended up offering to put my name forward…

ADRIEN: Another Hedgehog?!

BERNARD: Yes…

ADRIEN: He doesn't have a name?

BERNARD: Of course. Is there a problem?

ADRIEN: Not at all…

BERNARD: And so, my name was eventually put forward…

ADRIEN: By Roland Chicamour. Eventually put forward by Roland Chicamour.

BERNARD: That's right, by Roland Chicamour, yes… And when I told you this, I was hoping, perhaps naively, that you'd rejoice that the chance currents of life were drawing us closer together…

ADRIEN: The chance currents of life?!

BERNARD: Absolutely! Well! Not only did you not really rejoice, now you're telling me that if I dare so much as set foot in your club, you'll leave...

ADRIEN: You can go or not, it'll make no difference to my decision to leave...

BERNARD: That's even worse. Just me being a member at all makes you want to get out!

ADRIEN: 'The chance currents of life'... Is that what you call brown-nosing Chicamour for three solid months so he'd put your name forward?

BERNARD: What do you mean? We fell in together and got on! When you spend time with Chicamour you're a model of tolerance, but when I do the same I'm an arse-licker, is that it? You should be pleased that I've ended up seeing a better side of him. It proves I've learned from you...you've made me more forgiving; some of my sharper edges have been smoothed off.

ADRIEN: Look, it's Thursday evening, let's meet up at the weekend and sort all this out.

BERNARD: Come to this dinner with me.

ADRIEN: I can't.

BERNARD: Come on, let's go...

ADRIEN: No...

BERNARD: (*Dragging him by the arm.*) Yes! Come on! Get going! And yes for the weekend.

ADRIEN: (*Freeing his arm.*) You don't get it, I'm not coming this evening...I'm not going.

BERNARD: It's you who doesn't get it. Either you come or...

ADRIEN: Or what?

BERNARD: Or you come.

ADRIEN: Anyway I can't come, I've got a date here at half ten.

BERNARD: Here, at half ten?

ADRIEN: (*Amused.*) Yes...I'm being picked up.

BERNARD: You're being picked up...

ADRIEN: Yeah...a girlfriend.

BERNARD: A girlfriend?

ADRIEN: Yes. Are you going to keep repeating everything I say? ... A young woman – who I'm seeing – at the moment – Anne, she's called – Anne Belmont – she's thirty-five – she's divorced – I knew her before, I lost touch with her while she was married. We bumped into each other again and...and there you go! Maybe you were right...

BERNARD: Meaning?

ADRIEN: I don't know... Happiness and all that...meeting someone... It's not a gift or a talent...maybe it is just a question of luck... We're getting on really well, you know?

Pause. BERNARD is stunned.

BERNARD: Well, look, no problem...give her a ring... She can come and get you there, after the dinner. That way I can meet her. We could go for a drink, just the three of us!

ADRIEN: Yeah but no.

BERNARD: Why not?! Why are you being so pig-headed? There must be a way round this. You might make an effort! Have you any idea of the effort I'm making here not to take this as an absolutely terminal insult? The effort I'm making to salvage something between us!

ADRIEN: And have you any idea of the effort I've been making, every single morning for the last three months, not to howl with laughter when you come moping in here with a face like a slapped walrus?! If we go out for a drink, the three of us, what do I say to my girlfriend? Darling, this is Bernard, that's right, that Bernard, my partner, my mate, yes, father of the three little princesses, lucky husband of the lovely Léo... Like a brother to me, that's right... There... Is that what I'm going to say?

BERNARD: Well, perhaps not quite so... [*over the top.*]

ADRIEN: Ah but no. I can't say that because when I talk to her about you, that's not the sort of thing I say. Would you like to know the sort of thing I say when I talk about you?

BERNARD: Okay, okay, so perhaps we won't go for a drink.

ADRIEN: No, perhaps we won't.

BERNARD: But you could still call her and tell her to pick you up after the dinner.

ADRIEN: No. And you better call and tell them you're running late. It'd be a mite stupid to get kicked out of the club before you actually get in. (*He buries himself in his work again.*)

BERNARD: Adrien…Adrien, I'm holding my hand out to you, I'll forget everything… I'm asking you to come with me.

A long silence. ADRIEN shakes BERNARD's hand and disappears into his work again. BERNARD sighs and leaves with heavy tread. Pause. He comes back.

And may I ask what exactly you do tell your 'fiancée' when you can bring yourself to talk about me? … You know, just because we're business partners doesn't mean I can't sack you…

ADRIEN: Partners with a sacred bond…

BERNARD: Get up now, follow me out of here, and it's all over… We'll forget all about it…

ADRIEN: Do you remember the day you asked me to put your name forward? Babette called and she had a tantrum on the phone. You wouldn't give in…for her own good…a 'lesson'…you can't just throw a wobbly and get what you want in this life… And at that exact moment, you were doing exactly the same thing… You were throwing a wobbly, a big sulky fit… And I didn't want to give in either, for your own good… I thought we'd talk about it calmly the next day…and then I'd be quite happy to put you forward…if you were still keen… But then, yes, really, the chance currents of life… We just happened to bump into Chicamour at the restaurant where we were meeting Legrand for lunch… when I saw you giving him a bear-hug and lighting his big fat cigar for him… I was sorry, I was truly sorry not to have said yes to you before… Because then, it was too late… You were pathetic… It was humiliating…

BERNARD: I didn't light his cigar, I just lent him my lighter.

ADRIEN: And since then, I live in hope every single day that you'll wake up and see what's happening to you; and every single day I watch you sinking lower and lower...

BERNARD: He looked so sad! We were toasting our deal in Champagne and he was all on his own in a corner... What was I supposed to do? Cut him dead? We'd just snatched a very big contract out from under him, it was doing the decent thing to offer him a drink... I'm not one to kick a man when he's down.

ADRIEN: Chicamour's never been down in his life. Anyway, it's one thing not to kick him, it's something else altogether to... Oh forget it...

BERNARD: No, no, go on, something else altogether to what?

ADRIEN: Oh Bernard, if someone had told us this story about somebody else we'd have pissed ourselves.

BERNARD: What story?

ADRIEN: Why has this happened to us? What's going on?

BERNARD: What are you talking about?

ADRIEN: You know what I'm talking about!

BERNARD: No I don't. I don't know what Chicamour's told you...

ADRIEN: Chicamour hasn't told me anything... Is there something to tell?

BERNARD: You're the one who...

ADRIEN: I haven't seen Chicamour since the last Hedgehog dinner. A month ago. Léo told me.

BERNARD: You… [*see each other*]?

ADRIEN: We meet up sometimes.

BERNARD: So?

ADRIEN: So nothing. We meet, we talk, I talk to her…and she talks to me…

BERNARD: What has she…?

ADRIEN: Well…

Pause.

BERNARD: I didn't know it was going to be that sort of thing.

ADRIEN: You didn't know that Chicamour organizes…

BERNARD: He asked us round for dinner.

ADRIEN: You're lying.

BERNARD: I misunderstood.

ADRIEN: Léo didn't know, but you certainly did.

BERNARD: Well since Léo apparently tells you everything, you'll know we stayed five minutes max and then got out of there.

ADRIEN: Bernard, I'm not telling you off because you went to a bit of a swinger's party with Léo! What on earth would that have to do with me?

BERNARD: That's what I'd like to know… And I'll be asking Léo.

ADRIEN: You know bloody well what Léo thought. And you know bloody well that she's absolutely right.

BERNARD: I don't know what Léo thinks about anything. I'm sure she's told you she never says a word to me anymore.

ADRIEN: She thinks…she thought, anyway, because I think I've managed to persuade her you didn't know where you were taking her…she thought that you'd tried to…to offer her to Chicamour.

BERNARD: Offer her?

ADRIEN: Offer her…a little present…to go with the Havana cigars and the case of Chablis.

Pause. BERNARD shakes his head but can't think of anything to say.

The touching thing about it is, she admitted to me that she was okay to play along. Until she realised you were planning to leave her one-on-one with the master of ceremonies.

BERNARD: Play along how?

ADRIEN: Well… The swinging thing… Take part. With you… She thought maybe you…needed something a bit…to get you…

BERNARD: I see, she really does tell you everything…

ADRIEN: Well who's she supposed to talk to?

BERNARD: Right, as far as I understand it, you have in-depth discussions with my wife about my sexual shortcomings, so what do you say about me to your tart?

ADRIEN: To who?

BERNARD: This new…you know, this stupid slag who's dropping in around half ten for a shag on the desk!

ADRIEN: No, no… No, Bernard, I'm not having you talking like that…

BERNARD: Oh really?

ADRIEN: No.

BERNARD: And why not?

ADRIEN: Because I'm going to give you a smack in the face.

BERNARD: She's not a stupid slag?

ADRIEN: No.

BERNARD: She must be… That's all you ever knock off… What? Love of your life, is she? Going to get married? Big deal! Your first wife was a bit of a stupid slag too, wasn't she?

ADRIEN throws his glass of water in BERNARD's face. Silence. Then BERNARD calmly picks up his own glass and throws it in ADRIEN's face. Pause. Water dripping down their faces. ADRIEN goes into the wash-room. We hear running water.

ADRIEN: (*Off.*) Bernard?

BERNARD: Yeah?

ADRIEN appears in the bathroom door.

ADRIEN: All right?

BERNARD: You?

ADRIEN: Oh… (*Pause.*) I do know why the dinners were so important to me. For one night a month, it was like I had the right to just hang out with people, just be with

people without particularly respecting them or admiring
them. Your dentist Boulanger, he's bitter and a bit of
an arse, frankly, but when he laughs, it... I don't know.
Same with the others. And I don't suppose they rate
me much either but just once every now and then they
like to see me. Hi Addy! Hiya Chippy! Seen Roly?
He's chatting with Winky...sitting in the cave in a circle
round the fire. I couldn't last a single day working in
the same office with them, but just once a month, it
was a way of... And just that one time a month I was
guaranteed an evening where there was absolutely no
chance whatsoever of bumping into someone like you...

Pause. BERNARD stunned

Léo's leaving you too. She told me she'd told you... All
this over a tie.

*ADRIEN goes back into the bathroom. BERNARD loosens his
tie and takes it off over his head without untying it. He
follows ADRIEN into the bathroom.*

BERNARD: (*Off.*) This is absurd... Put this tie on and go...

*We hear a blow, BERNARD is catapulted out of the
bathroom, tie in hand.*

Go on... (*Heads back towards the bathroom, holding his
tie like a halter.*) For me... Pop this tie on (*Goes into
bathroom.*) Go on...

ADRIEN: (*Off. Beside himself.*) Will you just fuck off!

BERNARD: (*Off.*) What? Slip this tie on and we'll say no
more about it... There we are... Who's a pretty boy
then?

ADRIEN: (*Off.*) Bernard, get your hands off...

BERNARD: (*Off.*) Just straighten it for you...let me do this...
Let me! ... There... Now let's get it nice and tight shall
we?

ADRIEN: (*Off. Fear in his voice.*) Wait, Bernard, it's a bit
airless in here...we should get out... Stop it...!

BERNARD: (*Off.*) It's your tie...

ADRIEN: (*Off.*) Give over with the tie...

BERNARD: (*Off.*) ...it's your club, you're right, go on, you'd
better get round there...

ADRIEN: (*Off.*) ...Bernard, let's nip out for a quick drink,
what do you say? ... GET OFF!

BERNARD: (*Off.*) ...you'd better get going, what fun you'll
have...

We hear a dull blow.

That's enough!

Another blow.

Stop that!

We hear a sharp slap.

ADRIEN: (*Off.*) Bernard!

*Sound of a struggle. Breaking glass. Heavier and heavier
blows. ADRIEN groaning.*

Ah, my ear...my ear...

BERNARD: (*Off. Between gritted teeth.*) Let's do this tie up nice
and tight... That's it... That's it... Now, keep still! Keep
still, little Hedgehog, don't you prick me...

A faint groan from ADRIEN.

KEEP STILL! Nice and tight! … That's it, what a handsome chap, that's right… There!

A silence which gets longer and longer. Eventually BERNARD reappears looking as if a burden has been lifted from him. He puts out the office light and ADRIEN's desk lamp. The only light in the room is now the glow from the street and the headlights of passing cars. He dials a number.

Hello, poppet, it's Daddy here… Not in bed? … Can you put Mummy on…? Oh. How long ago? … Who's looking after you then? … Oh I see, and are your sisters in beddy-byes? … No sweetie, hands can't walk about on their own… Because it's impossible, darling, a hand is attached to an arm which is attached to a body… Go to sleep, poppet… Well that's what's called a severed hand, but a severed hand can't move and you can't possibly have seen one run across your bed… No cutie-pie, there are no severed hands, no witches, no dark shadow… My love, don't think about things like that, you're only six, death is a long way off, a very long way off, it doesn't exist, poppet, it doesn't mean anything, honestly… A long way! Further away than the moon… Even further than that! … No, no ghosts either… All right, but you have to promise to be good… Okay, here we go: five…four…three… Yes, I love you… All right start again: (*He counts gently.*) Five…four…three…two… one… What? … No, there's no such thing as the Devil either, Darling, no such thing as the Devil… (*He hangs up, thinks for a moment then dials again.*) No, not 666. (*Dials again.*) Ah, yes, hello… Police please… What? Yes, yes, I'll bear with you… (*Pause.*) Ah, yes hello, I'm calling really because I've just… I've just eliminated a friend and… Sorry? … No, I've just killed someone, you see... I'm at my office with the...other party... With the corpse... No well, I'm calling to say you'd better come and get us. I don't know the procedure but I suppose the best thing would be a police car and an ambulance or, well, a vehicle for my friend... Yes, so, my name is...

A noise comes from the bathroom. BERNARD freezes.
ADRIEN coughs.

Just a moment, um, actually no... What? ... Yes I know it's a serious matter but, in actual fact, I think I've made a bit of a mistake... I don't think he's dead... I know what you're saying but there's really no need... Look, you didn't shout at me when I told you I was a murderer so I don't see why you should now! ...

ADRIEN appears carrying a bottle of water. His neck's a mess...

(*Still on the phone.*) Well you just do what you bloody like!

He hangs up. ADRIEN drinks and gets his breath back.
Silence.

Adrien...

ADRIEN: (*Has virtually no voice but makes up for it with imperious gestures.*) Don't move! ... Stay where you are...!

ADRIEN puts the light on, opens the window and leans out for air. BERNARD gets the tie from the bathroom.

Put that tie down!

BERNARD: (*Advancing on him.*) You have to do it for me.

ADRIEN: (*Snatching up a chair for protection.*) Put down the tie and step away!

BERNARD: (*Knotting the tie round his own neck.*) Go on...
Squeeze! You have to go through what I've been
through.

ADRIEN: What you've been through?!

BERNARD: I see it all now.

ADRIEN: Stay where you are!

BERNARD: You have to feel what I felt... The violence...
First let me take you in my arms and then – go for it!
(*He tightens the tie round his own neck.*) You must!

ADRIEN: No! Look, you've got to get help...

BERNARD: But no, that's just it, I don't anymore! I'm
finding out where the whole thing comes from... I see
it all now. Our friendship has never seemed so real, so
alive as during those few minutes when I thought you
were dead...

ADRIEN: Bernard, look, I was really scared, that really hurt;
it still hurts and I'm still really scared!

BERNARD: You mustn't be scared. You're my friend! ... I
know it for sure now. For sure! You can do anything you
like to me; do your worst, it just doesn't matter. That's
the certainty I want you to feel as well. Unless you kill
me, you'll never feel for me what I feel for you. (*He
holds the end of the tie out to ADRIEN.*) Please... Kill me, go
on...make us quits... Come on! (*He tugs the tie violently.*)

ADRIEN: No more killing. Not tonight, no more killing. All
right?

BERNARD: But why?

ADRIEN: Because it's dangerous.

BERNARD: Trying to stay one up, are you?

ADRIEN: Let's go for a drink.

BERNARD: So you refuse to do as I ask?

ADRIEN: I'm asking you to come for a drink.

BERNARD: Scared, are you?

ADRIEN: I'm thirsty.

BERNARD: You won't even try and kill me because you're scared you won't feel anything... You don't really give a toss about me – that's the truth you're scared to face!

ADRIEN: I'm going...

BERNARD: What about the girlfriend? Are you not going to wait for her?

ADRIEN: What I'm saying, I need to have a drink with a mate, all right... (*He shivers.*) I'm cold.

BERNARD: It's the shock, the reaction.

ADRIEN: I'm really, really cold.

BERNARD takes his coat off and covers ADRIEN with it.

BERNARD: But after...you promise?

ADRIEN: (*Shivering.*) After, we'll see... I want a drink.

BERNARD goes to tie his scarf round ADRIEN's neck.
ADRIEN yells in fear.

BERNARD: There should be champagne left in the fridge. (*BERNARD goes to look.*) This is really important, Adrien, I'm not messing about.

ADRIEN: Take that tie off...you look grotesque.

BERNARD: But how will you...?

ADRIEN: I'll manage... A tie isn't strictly necessary...

BERNARD: Well, I've given you fair warning. If you don't do it I'll never forgive you as long as I live. If you don't kill me you're dead!

END.

www.ingramcontent.com/pod-product-compliance
Ingram Content Group UK Ltd.
Pitfield, Milton Keynes, MK11 3LW, UK
UKHW020728280225
455688UK00012B/554